LEDGER OF CROSSROADS

POEMS

LEDGER OF CROSSROADS

JAMES BRASFIELD

Louisiana State University Press

Baton Rouge

Published by Louisiana State University Press
Copyright © 2009 by James Brasfield
All rights reserved
Manufactured in the United States of America

AN LSU PRESS PAPERBACK ORIGINAL
First printing

Designer: Barbara Neely Bourgoyne
Typefaces: Vendetta Medium, text; Gotham, display
Printer and binder: Thomson-Shore, Inc.

LIBRARY OF CONGRESS
CATALOGING-IN-PUBLICATION DATA

Brasfield, James.
   Ledger of crossroads : poems / James Brasfield.
   p. cm.
   ISBN 978-0-8071-3520-4 (pbk. : alk. paper)
   I. Title.
   PS3552.R32755L43 2009
   811'.6—dc22

                              2009012308

Grateful acknowledgment is made to the following publications in which poems in this book first appeared:*Agni, Antaeus, Colorado Review, Crazyhorse, Heliotrope, The Iowa Review, Kestrel, The Literary Review, The New Virginia Review, Poetry Wales, Prairie Schooner, The Roanoke Review, Quarterly West, The Southern Review,* and *Sou'wester.* "Celan" and *"The Chair and the Pipe"* were republished in the online magazine *Poetry Daily.* "Celan" was reprinted in *Poetry Daily: 366 Poems from the World's Most Popular Poetry Website* (Diane Boller, Don Selby and Chryss Yost, editors). "Identities" and "The Renovation" were reprinted in *Imported Breads: Literature of Cultural Exchange* (Phillip Sterling, editor). Special thanks to the Council for International Exchange of Scholars for two Fulbright grants to Ukraine, where some of these poems were first drafted, and to the National Endowment for the Arts and the Pennsylvania Council on the Arts for grants that afforded me time to complete a number of poems in this book.

To Charlotte

CONTENTS

I

Identities

I stand on the end platform of the tram and am completely
unsure of my footing in this world . . . I can see the whole ridge
of the whorl of her right ear and the shadow at the root of it.
—FRANZ KAFKA

1

Another night, another packed trolley
approaches through rain—
all those faces at the windows,
taking the wide curve slowly
over the puddled street
rising, reflecting scattered lights
around the square.
                              The wheels rumble—
their distant squeak and heavy scraping.
I don't need to see sparks fly to know
electricity's out there. The Dnieper's
dark width curves around the hip of Podol.
The Black Sea waits, but I'm not so sure
about the moon and stars I've not seen
in weeks, even late, coming back to my room,
to the Westclox I wind daily
for its iambs, downbeat
for the stray dogs barking.

The word is out, Another hard winter
is on the way. Man-made or not,
it is not enough to say, It is all just
in the planet's revolving on its axis.

2

In Moscow, red Parisian fish
by Matisse, *Goldfish,*
wait in the master's cylindrical bowl
flanked by arrangements
of flowers and plants
that just might paper the wall.
In that borrowed world
abstract strokes at the surface
are reflections of fish,
their eyes open in the clear water
upright and still on the round table
balanced on two thin legs
with no allusion to a third—
all cropped between the curved arm of a chair
and pink blossoms on the black floor.

3

In Kyiv, citizens decipher the surface
as at the Pole, an Eskimo
reads snow, as in Baltimore a man
might read the *Sun* in that Southern city
where *The Blue Nude* reclines, framed
behind a pane of glass. She might be
anywhere, come back, too cold
from shadows set high in deep perspective.

She contemplates the singularity
in her right arm and hand,
turned parallel to her body—not time
nor place, but these very parts of her,
like the semicircles of the vegetation,
like the circles of her breasts. . . .

A chair set out on the beach at night,
a seat on the crowded trolley
about to stop, or the chair in Moscow
might be hers.
                    We can see
the sensation that she feels,
the moment of our being in her stare.

The Chair and the Pipe

(van Gogh)

Leaves come cured and shredded.
I ignite them, inhale them.
Blood totes them through the heart.

Smoke curls from the charred bowl
and from my lungs, turns
just above the olive grove, vanishes.

Crows circle high over the trees.
Where to from this little yellow house?
Snow falls, each flake a crystal petal.

Each branch gathers up its layer.
Seeds from the sunflower
lie eclipsed in the frostburnt herbs.

Today, at one stroke of my brush
wind threw shadows from my pipe—dry shards
closing my eyes. Theo, I saw

the still deeper shades of black
unending. Think of the sacks of ash
I could have worked into garden, field, and sky.

The Renovation

Late, by the whitewashed wall
of the eighteenth-century church,
a gray afternoon is committed to flames.
An old woman sweeps the courtyard.
A black scarf hides her head.

She stops, warms her hands
by the fire from the renovation,
from parceled trunks of chestnut
and maple, which yesterday
cast shadows on the wall.

For centuries she's swept the leaves
with her broom of birch twigs and straw.
From the court of Macbeth, men
in heavy coats and fedoras
stoke the fire with Styrofoam.

The fire flares in the rain.
Through white smoke, black smoke
rises, passing columns
and arches. A raven trails
a hooded crow to the courtyard.

A magpie rests in the scaffolding
of branches of the broadest oak.
I swear by the old woman, the earth,
by the deepening pools of water,
by the gold eyes of the black goat—

by the brown loaves of bread
I swear by St. Agatha's breasts

the magpie has flown six hundred years
from Lubart's castle, from the siege
of dilapidation at Lutsk,

from apple tree, from pig squeal
and cockcrow, all those deserted
factories by the river Styr.
But here, gone the dark birds,
the men and the woman

who will return, who have always
returned to fewer trees and a wall.
The magpie waits hunched on a branch.
Ashes to wind dissolve in rain,
in the sound and glow of the fire

dying out, then the flapping,
the black wings of the magpie. . . .
Flow on, Dnieper, south of here the stars
open out, like old charred bones
kicked across an orchard path.

Close enough to feel the warmth,
I breathe the smoke from the fire.
When I close my eyes I can almost
hear the Scythians dancing—
the lute and drum and bells.

Kyiv

The Anatomy of Nostalgia

The gray light that is dusk, the mist
that gathers at the end of August,
the sudden drop of warmth in the coming dark,
the stillness of an arclight over the dim road,
and farther still, lamplight at a window,

the curtains drawn—there, a woman
puts a small supper at the table, pours
flavored water from a crystal carafe,
an heirloom like a root toward the river.
The stewed apple slices have darkened from days
of floating in the green jar.

And the man pours himself a vodka,
the first of many, and cuts the bread.
Tomorrow remains so far off.
Its burdens are as yesterday's.

I know these things
from sitting at the table,
from walking the road. I know them
from a train passing through a town at night,
the wet streets, the dim station,
the streets again and another house

outside of town, the darkness everywhere
filling in the impossible space
a light is assigned, yet always a road
at dusk, the mist, the arclight
a hundred yards before the next,

and the road to a path through the forest,
a light at a window as if only
a light burned among the trees—
a candle on the chest of a corpse, at nightfall.

Perigee

January. Again the abandoned nest
snowcapped in the young maple—
red tipped branches timed to bud

as rain taps. Wind shakes this hilltop
corner house, as if it were
some drafty lugger. And in the hearth,

the soot-covered vault a mausoleum,
balled newspaper, heart of the kindling,
split lengths of oak and maple on the grate.

I move the match flame from place to place.
Days are columns of smoke up the flue.
I'm at sea and the house creaks.

The heart bursts through the stack,
a beacon, a pyre on the beach.
First, reflected light, diffused—

small flames climbing the quartered tiers,
then the sound of flames, their contagion,
the wheeze of burning, the bark snapping.

From grooved fibers come
screets of a bird calling, a maple's
or oak's memory of a tenant's morning

and the rising chant of insects. Logs swell.
Spiked shadows fly through the firescreen,
then the shrill repetitions,

as if stowed away in burning crates,
the migration freed
in a combinatoria of frenzy—calls,

one or two I recognize yet can't
remember, released to the wet air
from the aviary of smoke. They sing

till fire takes the heap.
The operatic backdrop lights the room.
I feel the heat sound makes.

Orange cinders fall through the grate
like isinglass crystals to ash.
The inward night is fire is sea is home.

I think of birds over water.
No limbs, tree hollow,
no remembrance of leaves—

never to come down,
gray birds cross the mountains of the moon.
The windows rattle at this address.

From the Ledger of Crossroads

The dead, the disappeared, the desperate—
a steel blue sky, snow fine as dust,
almost smoke in a place of no time.
Though the world of the open well, of the horsecart
passes, passing deepens: Black Death, famine,
broadsword and pike, sten-gun and bayonet,
singular passings of each who was,
who might have been, who is:
there is no end to history.
Each potato is held and peeled. Years now,
people have carted potatoes
only so far, to the trains to Kyiv.

Whiteness covers all, nights and days
alive with the static of centuries,
each year its ledger of decrees. But there are those,
each in their uprootedness,
who, like the oil lamp hung above a table,
surround themselves with imperishable air,
who rekindle luminosity
and in their inmost rooms piece together
the incompatible from floors littered
with smutty shards. Then shadows
stand at junctures of connection. Stars
ferry the weight on extended shoulders.

And they are strangers who walk dark streets,
snow rippling over the loud curve of tram tracks.
Blocks away, Tatars crossed the Dnieper—impatient
hooves entered the water. Depths silenced them,
then Asia was here, the city sacked, then the dead,
the disappeared, the desperate—remembered,

recorded, the anonymous enrolled through seasons
of noise. Hooded crows and ravens gathered in
the chestnut trees, bare-leafed or full, shadowing
the buried tributary beneath the street
branching from the avenue along the river. There
the wise Iaroslav bathed at that gentle confluence.

And those birds in momentary
constellations are not less than legend.
Iaroslav is dust. Dust collects on the marble
sarcophagus at the church of St. Sophia,
near the cobble street where I witnessed
a pine coffin lifted atop a Lada.
A man with a hammer ran from his apartment
and reaching up, nailed down the lid.
A raven strolled back and forth
on that narrow street. Stray dogs
were forming packs again. Everywhere,
chestnut petals were falling.

MacDougal Street

in memory of Joseph Brodsky

I've come to find you among the faces
at this poor-man's Venetian café.
Below pressed-tin patterns on the ceiling,
a stucco arch is, as if of St. Petersburg,
the prominent architectural detail.
Under the grimy cornices, a rendition of
the Quattrocento hangs broadly framed,
a life-moment casual as a wrinkled shirt.

I think of you, back to the wall
at a marble table, a man conscious
to keep the maudlin at bay,
folding a cocktail napkin
into the shape of a bird,
passing off some deft remark—
Ya, this unavoidable muck of things
seems nothing new, thus this place must be real.

So best not to translate swallow as sparrow,
as if birds were the same in a target language,
better to see a swallow framed by rooftops,
darting over some Leningrad street, though
a sparrow here comes closest to the neighborhood
where flies are everywhere by early summer.
Thus your worldview was obstinate,
a stoic's pleasure at saying no.

It was a task being a taskmaster
for Cyrillic script, then for the Roman, *en face*,
your Audenesque American take ever at work,
your mending order of words, the draftsman's

conversation—your lines drawn from the ground,
steps measured from vanishing points
with your day's wash strung from marble posts,
with a breeze to make the laundry sway.

This afternoon across the street
from 44 Morton, the tulip tree was blooming.
Sidewalk cracks branched like routes on a trampled map.
Broken by history, concrete keeps
its jagged sides all the way to the corner
where you stopped, looked over your shoulder,
then turned to Seventh Ave., not a heaven,
as if a place could be such.

Joseph, the wolves still hunt you, eager to lower
your plane of regard. Now, no matter the pack's size,
time stands in its way, no longer your terror
of anticipation—to reiterate
or retaliate—or the tragedy clear
in your contemplation on the edge of it.
It is better to derive life from the poem
than the poem from life, even in a crowded café.

Yeah, each year for you marked an *anno Domini*.
A man lives in a city. It becomes a place
for him, if only a tautology. New York
and Venice comprised your lost Petropolis,
but there are no windows in death to look from.
Life has only windows on the dying and the dead.
A live thing that's frightened, a bird is
a consoling thing. Like art, each survives in form.

II

Necessary Days

What has been called, is still called, a modern man
                    from a mercantile place—
          I am in the forest, in that circumference,

a previous nature that has survived
                    and may still, though I understand
          the changes, even here: land cleared

for cabins, for someone like me
                    this compromised space
          to move deeper on a blazed trail,

to think about what around me
                    is yet unaltered by others and thus
          reaches back, before the stone wall

or a split-rail fence—a vision of being
                    I could not have unless I am
          here, looking back, now.

How strange to know this—
                    that I want to hear for a long time
          only sounds of an isolated moment,

in deep woods, and later to hear
                    a Brahms cello sonata, knowing
          how the two fuse ignites the fire of hours,

how silence, the music of it waiting,
                    carried me here through the traffic
          of necessary days in the modern world,

a domain dead set to cross the borders
                    of relevance, to make it loud with
          the idiot music of another nature.

Heart of Dixie

Every day came, the char of silence and beauty,
brick foundations of what was here, dirt roads
cut through pines, rivers and the dust of the dead,
bone silt and a song, bird cries, the freight train

through the county, crops and cows, chickens wandering
a patch of yard, wind through sun-silvered leaves,
the clay baked hard, undulating in August, farmers
in a field, weathered wooden sheds, isolated.

Every day came, a hound in the yard.
Call it circumstances, the way we thought things
had to be, rough and polished stones on a creek bank.
We had no choice but to believe, sincere and alone

and the black faces, their eyes lowered
in our homes on Broad Street. We did not sympathize.
It was almost normal. Call it circumstance,
the alarm and nature of sidelong glances,

the way we thought things had to be,
God's will, our history and we wanted it quiet.
It was always dark. You get used to anything, we said
with eyes lowered. It was almost perfect here,

mist and wildflowers, the charred cross
in a field. It was almost normal, a quiet stream
and a gravel road. Every day came.
It was dark and no one could see.

The Illness, 1960

O Spirits of whom my soul is but a little finger,
Direct it to the lid of its flesh-eye.
—JEAN TOOMER

July in Alabama,
fresh water in a bedpan,
a marble-top table,
pills and thermometer,
lamplight by the bed: I'm a boy
with *The Rime of the Ancient Mariner.*
Like a stowaway I inhabit
the boxwood engravings by Doré.
My wooden model of the Santa Maria
sails the striped folds
of the white chenille spread.

                     High fever
from what I don't know; Dr. Bledsoe says
if I do not eat I will be fed—
a needle, a tube for the arm.
The cook, Flo, brings cornbread and broth,
I not eating, the doctor adding, "Don't
get up without someone's help"—
and later, after help to the john,
I'm back on board the tall bed,
my ruddy face
abandoned in the mirror.
Grandmother with a wet cloth daubs
my lips, my cheeks, my brow—
then the Polar Spirits of an alcohol rub,
and crushed-ice spoonfed slowly.
Outside the open windows
cars travel the hill, their lights
turning the room in shadows.

For a time,
friends with cap pistols pop the dark.
The water-snakes, the cottonmouths of Eufaula
circle my bed, and I not eating
and the Santa Maria
and the Mariner's barque
become one ship on the gray current
glinting, and Doré's DEATH
and LIFE-IN-DEATH casting dice,
the parched men dying on deck,
here the Mariner,
the great white bird hung around his neck,
and the darkness of my ship heaving
and setting on the swells,
and I am hot as if standing at a fire,
unable to step away.
How hot, hot,
though long sheer curtains
move in the breeze and Grandfather
reading in the next room,
this his house of many doors,
and I know he is close to harbor
when under his door
light goes out, and he
near the edge of earth
has closed his issue of *Field and Stream,*
placed it on his bedside table,
not knowing he is foundering
already in the irons of cancer
where landfall's a grave near my father's
in this town on a bluff
where the doctor will sleep,
not waking to a call.

                    Hundreds of miles
to our small house, dark, near the sea,
I know my mother is crying to my father
to look in on us
and pleads with God that only
if she were dead . . .
but I, believing
in my father's duration as long as I live,
believing he sees what remains,
ask the dark if he is suffering, seeing us
here from that distant place.
Morning comes.
                        Flo brings a bowl of ice,
cornbread and broth.
                        I tell her thanks,
letting the food sit—
the fever breaking
and soon I'm calling for help to the john,
no one coming, and desperate I slide from my berth.
I stand and step as if toward shore,
as if up and down
in a high tide ebbing
and arrive and relieve myself
of what there is
to be relieved. I shower and dress.
I walk out on the warm floor,
neither a new world
nor the world I left.
I walk as one free from a closed country
to the sunlit kitchen. I eat
with Flo at the enamel-top table.

Waynesboro

Through the colonnades of oak
arched over the cold road, I drive through rain
filtered through the moss cathedral—
the outbound sun, distant at the crossing,

night, a large cloud, fills the air.
I remember my last spring here,
the air warm with the coming of another season.
Nothing was in the field, then a tent appeared

and a cross nailed to a sign. There
I witnessed the Pentecostal fire.
Fifty chairs circled a low stage
and two poles held the canvas high.

Four bare bulbs lit that tabernacle.
With a tambourine, Lurleen, our go-between,
beat out a rhythm on her thigh.
"Pray for me, I pray for you," she chanted,

while the organist moved from chord
to chord, holding each a long time.
The small clamor of hands clapping
was meant to stir the air in hell.

But who heard the wind rising
through sycamores, shifting the paunches
of the flaps, or past the hymns, the field,
miles away the serene code

of successive beats upon the tracks....
Yet what I remember most about Waynesboro,
governed still by its white grandees,
is an old woman, black, standing alone

on a hillside, watching from scrub grass,
waiting as the last passenger
run between Savannah and Atlanta
approached town, not to stop here,

never having stopped here, its whistle
like salvation blaring only nearer
before it was gone. Forever for me
she stands there, facing that train

as now on this road the dark, inbound
stillness trails the long freight of light.
She stands there, like the eternal
white sun over a tin-roofed shack.

Mechanical blades beat time, sweeping
rain from the glass. She is here—
borne up motionless above the crossties,
a place in mind, through the moonless night.

Passage

Past sweet gum, oak, pecan, past mimosa,
past pine, magnolia along the highway—
honeysuckle on a barbed wire fence . . .
And the convicts, working in clean white pants
and open shirts on a summer morning,
the blue stripe loud down each pants leg—
they laid brick, building a small house.
The guard in a new uniform
sat and watched from a makeshift shed,
his shotgun balanced across his knees.
So many times we have seen this together
and the soiled dusk of those days.
Imagine one of those men moving far back
and parallel to the road, instinctively
stopping to clean his wound, edging on
through the evening as it darkens,
through the gradual and deepening tangle
of brush and trees. His movement marks him
while the night hides him in its cool
reprieve. Yet when he can no longer
hold back sleep, he will dream his crimes.
Think of this man as we turn now
toward the particulars that come to us
after years together. The unlenitive past
cannot hold us. We are each upon the road
again in our separate passage. And though
the man that I have given you lies in darkness,
tomorrow's route charts itself, pent
with his compass fear, beneath his closed eyes.

Pietàs

All night behind the cabin, the tall pine
creaked slowly, like an I-beam twisting.

Today, wind through the trees, oceanic—
treetops have the sound of dry leather

bending—the dead beech
a rusty gate-hinge opening . . .

wind hurrying the ice to freeze
the creek, the current narrowed—

leaves flow, each like a fish
making its way as it senses.

Paths of sunlight to the forest floor—fallen limbs
caught in the crooks of dead and living trees.

Woods

From fallen places, refugees seek
their lives among the trees.
One cares for oneself in a forest.

Later, the afterwards, felled
trees hauled off, stumps burned,
the ground is cultivated.

The seared gives way
to sun for a field and a flower
again, a garden.

We live among people
and know well the phrase,
dark forest of self.

We have tried to keep what remains
good in a forest: wild phlox
in the zone of possibilities,

pollen grain falling on stigma.
A day here or there, a silence
lives in each of us,

as in the mountain lion and its prey.
A physics lives in both. Each
survives by their bold moves.

They germinate in us.
A midsummer breeze through the forest,
birdsong, or garden chair, a book,

a flicker waddling across the lawn
are sanctuaries we surrender to,
yet no matter how

we see the woods, or live there,
there we remain strangers.
What is wild fends for itself.

But solitude can be compelled
under forest hemlocks
or by the hemlock hedge.

We sit under a pair of apple trees.
Woods were here, then a pasture.
Woods wait beneath us in the garden.

Tracks

Tonight the trolley returns you
to Kontraktova Square, close
to the place called your room—
not your home. So many years away,
never this far, so long a time . . .

You've always been at the edge of borders.
Here you have your shadow
cast by the dim light from the conductor's
compartment wall. Soon you'll unlock
the one night continuing, though days pass.

When your eyes close, your shadow
will lie down with you, will transfer
to morning, to keep you company,
your shadow with no one—not even
you to remember when it is gone.

                                    Kyiv

The Knobbed Whelk

for Leopold Staff

From sea grit, from increments of lime,
come determinations of shell and snail,
answer and riddle, suitcase and refugee,
the chambered shape an acute anatomy
for sound. Its propulsion inherited
a Braille history of predation, the slow drift
of passage. At the whorl I hear
cadential breaking from the mountains—
as if submerged, the route from Lvov
to Warsaw crossed high barrier reefs,
where ocean and gravity could not encumber
the whelk's arrival from its deep labor.
A late-comer to dry light, the shell survives,
sea-stained, flesh created, a heart,
its branches severed. As if from flame
the ribs now are streaks of dusk, sinews
of the outer hand, a palm cupping the dark.
An empty room around which days and nights gather.
This scant unusual basket, woven of lime,
a stone shawl. I set it down to see it.

Letter from Germany

for my father (1909–1952)

Many things have been done
And many hours merged into so many days
Since I last had time to write you.
It has rained all day and the blossoms
Have nearly all been beaten down.
The bareness and gray scud clouds
Add to the gloom. Cold rain
Keeps us aware that there is a war on.
With the wind behind it, the rain feels like
Someone slapping you with a wet towel.
And the mud is like Prairieville mud.
I was fooled last month,
It was pleasant and the fruit trees bloomed.
I fell to 145 pounds at the front
And I am somewhat embarrassed
The way my clothes drape about me.
I am on swing shift tonight.
Staring into the river, I quit thinking
For a while. I have this dream that I pass
A place called "Hotel Moderne":
I want to rent a room and don't have the time.
The first chance I get, I am going back.
It looked clean from the outside.
Last night I went to the USO show.
Three performers in an old building.
I felt sorry for them. The dancer
Couldn't dance for sour apples,
But got a big hand from the boys
Because she had so little on.
The comedian was good, the best

Was the old fellow who just sang.
He was not good. We wanted his songs
And he sang them. Tonight
There are flares and tracers, stories
Of paratroopers, but no sign of them.
I bought a doll finally for the little girl.
I didn't pay much, it was the best
I could find; there are more dolls' heads
Than dolls on the shelves. I have a radio
Now and get the news hot off the air
And real American jazz. I need
A particular big eyed, light hearted woman
To dance with. But she is not on this side
Of the Atlantic. Looking
At your picture, I have almost
Forgotten how you are. Alabama
Better have a big sweet potato crop
The year I come home. And get a bottle
Or two of bourbon stashed away
If you love me. It has been too long.
There is nothing normal left.
The smell of guns massed in this valley
Hangs bitter in the air.
A town burns across the ridge.
I know the distance. It is late,
And being out of candles, I have to quit.

Chernivtsi

Nor it nor no remembrance what it was.
—SHAKESPEARE, SONNET 5

Such weight, Little Vienna,
snow falling across Europe, villages
lost to avalanche. People who return
say the streets are clean in Deutschland—
on the walks, a mere light dusting

from the newly fallen. Here
in the crosswinds, streets
and walks are buried in ice.
Wherever they are, Little Vienna,
shovels wait shivering.

Last night, who spread the path
of ashes on the walk? Some new tenant
not knowing what else to do
with a cigar box of ashes, handed down,
found far back in the wardrobe?—

the new tenant happy after a night
of polka and a waltz, losing his feet
with his new wife, arm
in arm, and saying later, "Well,
there's this from yesterday?" . . .

Oh last night with stars scattered
across the blackest night—
ice giving way from the balconies . . .
The winter potatoes I peeled were stones
softening, deeply bruised.

Today, I'm nearly out of bread. Granules
of white mold brighten the heel of the brown loaf.
How those wisps of clouds closed in on the stars—
that sky now, a pale cotton curtain
about to fall from its string.

Already the path's covered as under a field
of crushed apples. Bags of ash wouldn't make
a foothold here where winter, as long
as snow falls, lasts a lifetime,
and not to remember the star lodged

in the branches, a crow now to light a limb,
and as it happens suddenly, those flocks
take flight. The gaps between them
are like those places where we hope to see
any star beneath moving clouds.

Does the old man hear those wings?—
in each hand a long poplar branch,
the knife-chipped tips probing
the furrowed millimeters of rippled ice—
or does the man leaning against the building

at the corner of Tolstoy Street?
He sings lightly to himself, staring
beyond the tin roofs, heavy with snow,
over the heraldic crests on the faded plaster
of your cracked facades, Little Vienna—

or bundled in black, returning to the village,
does the old woman under a scarf, sliding her feet
like a wind-up doll about to stop?
She leans into the knot end of a rope—
two bags of potatoes on a little wooden sled.

Celan

There,
the whisper:

gradual breath
fattens

a word, bud
of stem form—

never before
this one,

the return of
the recognizable.

The Blue Cottage

Still, it waits for you—
even in the dark you saw it clearly.
No fence claims it, no train for kilometers.
Light from its windows reached you
though it stands beyond the black pine
and birch forest, beyond the presence always
of the sudden storm and the narrow road.

Each evening, the return from work, mud, and ice,
you picked burs from your rough sheath.
Once, as a child, crossing the field, its green shoots
breaking through furrows, then the high meadow
of white clover, poppies and larkspurs,
you came to a small house near the river.
Blue shadows cooled the eaves of the hot thatch.

    Whoever lived there was away.
    You entered the yard. Past the peonies
    about to blossom, the roses in bloom, you pressed
    your open hands to the clean glass,
    resting your forehead on your spread fingers.
    Each point of touch was an island of flesh on the pane.
    You felt no fear, no anxiety of return.

    You looked into the shadows
    of the large room, the hearth's embers
    dying from the night fire.
    Sunlight gleamed on the plank table,
    the swept room spare, the crafted tools
    in their natural places, in what years
    had made for them by those who lived there.

In town, the organ grinder from Cologne
frightened you, his thick hands turning
the crank of the large box—the monkey
fitted in worn clothes, chained to the orchestrated—
that man so apart from the other, as if the animal
were not there as it leaped and danced on command.
Holding your mother's hand you thought of the house

in the meadow. You were looking out
at the gathered crowd even as they jostled you.
Whoever was with you is not here.
You lived on, after them—
that's all. Betrayal had only the moments
of significance you granted it.
Even those were a form of safekeeping.

The smallest animal of the forest
has itself and a place within as you
have made this space where the body
is touched gently by the desired.
The evidence of rain is its shimmer
on white clover, poppies and larkspurs.
Thunder does not frighten them.

By cadence, a man made this clear
upon words from the *Commedia* and passed
through the dark circumference
of trees. Like the house, his offering was
what couldn't be taken from a suitcase—
his measured landscape unlike your nightmare:
skittles spinning in a closed box....

> You saw bees return
> from the meadow to the hives

built for them under apple trees
beside the house. You learned
to see it by the small chimney
among the arms of willows.
Each shape came back to you—

each a release from suffering,
like oval stacks of hay
the morning your grandparents' shoulders
seemed ever lighter with each load
you tossed up—under the meadowlarks
jackrabbits leapt back and forth
across the field, no dog in sight.

So much was falling away
after surviving the hospital in autumn.
You knew, beyond the faint scent
of almond in the air and heavy clouds
funneling from earth into snowfall,
the current calmed within that distant
bend of the Vistula,

ultramarine in the shade, tips of leaves
breaking the tension of the surface—
there, your hair again, long enough to braid.
There were no tears left
for transport. Above that place,
summer knows no reprimand.
White clover, poppies and larkspurs remain.

The Replenishment

for Robert Motherwell

Line and plane are composed
wherever the gray squirrel
stops among the branches. It vaults
from spray to birch twigs shaken.

A bronze grackle settles in the dogwood—
the bird's yellow eyes are the shade of anthers
after flowers at the heart open.

In its moment, as when notched bracts,
those white petals, fall, the grackle
gathers itself up, its leave-taking arched
over the yard, then a cardinal's arrival,
flower to berry, the red drupe, a remnant
of style, centered in the passing crown.

When that bird enters dusk's orange plane,
I feel it's been too long since
someone spoke of consciousness.

Yet what was remains in the ultramarine
edged above this place—
in its cadmium green, an oval of gray,
a streak of vermilion
and the black smear perched
at the tip of the extended cadence.

A drip of paint seeks the natural event,
a contour of calligraphy, the mottled
shades of bark, where always for the moment,
the glance of yellow ochre.

Wherever I look in this window,
this is the end of winter
kernel and seed of the light divided.

IV

The Relief

Czernowitz

1

Lines of light are always: in them
you wait, anonymous part of what is seen,
where light within, as from an ikon,
radiates above the street. In these
second shadows cast, how true
the unchangeableness. You survive
a century of evenings, hours of the dark
as when a tide enters standing pools
high on a beach, and at dawn pulls back
having left what is found in the small impressions—
so your face no longer stands out
from the wall in darkness, yet
even at sunrise you have no face,
the mask, an open vault of air.

2

You watch over narrow N. Pryboya
Boulevard, not the strasse of
a hundred years ago. Who was
N. Pryboya? I believe Antschel
would remember the name of the strasse
and you outside my kitchen window,
your Hapsburg face faithful as daylight—
a silence without lament—more human
than of marble, more like a face carved
in an apple, dried, as if without withering.
Still, after so much, you have not
vanished along the way, your features
the blush of ripeness, a visibility
in relief—the lines of age unspoken.

3

(Of plaster: an Alpine belle from across the Danube, from a coat
of arms; a goddess from a temple along the Ganges or Tiber, or
pagan youth from a time above the Prut—your face, poised. A word
waits on your full lips, pursed lightly, lightly opened. Your eyes
are tapered shadows, cast in hollow sockets. Thick ribboned folds
crown your loose curls parted at the top of your wide brow and
gathered, crossing under the soft chin of your sculptured jaw—
your face framed by the balance of large leaves and wildflowers,
scrolled, branched and palmate, as from a tapestry brought into
relief from the half-oval base, the shape of a gravestone, above a
window. The effect is the height of flowering, or of flames—the
garden in early autumn or the fire in a hut on a Carpathian hill,
and you with no hands to rest your face in this eastern outpost,
its wind and its dust like an evening mist or a flurry of snow.)

4

Snow, crystalline under torch and arclight . . .
from plains into the mountains, hoofbeats, drums
over dirt streets and cobblestones, that long
parade: Scythian, Rus, Tatar and Turk,
black boots of Pole, Hussar, Romanian,
the Third Reich, *Homo Sovieticus* . . .
distances of villages, of cities,
determined by columns of smoke on the steppes—
What is the loss if your mask disappears?
Did your guise pass muster, was it overlooked
by Bolsheviks? Had it been from antiquity,
you'd've been shipped to Moscow, the bare brick
left unrepaired—incalculable the symptoms
of schism, no one will relieve your watch.

5

Those who saw you and see you no more;
those who have seen you for years, who know
of your face; those who glance up as if
staring at a tin can in the city dump;
those who see you for the first time
and each time after, who take your image,
your shadowed hollows, to the grave—
is it your mask those men and women,
buried here, mirror in the clear midnight
of the Resurrection, each plot its candle,
the sky smelling of wax? Hidden and apparent,
your expression is dry-eyed, set as a bride
who waits to marry her second husband
in the Palace of Solemn Events.

6

You stare over the cotton curtain
at my window. You look past me, past
my kitchen, vapor rising from my coffee—
your presence bright in the warmth of morning
sunlight. Below the gutter rusting
along the eaves, plaster falls away,
widening borders of exposed brick, threatening
your days mortared to the cracked facade.
Remember the boy Antschel running with hoop
and stick down the strasse, who, years later,
holding the hand of a girl, turned and kissed her
lightly under the veil of arclight—
of a long time ago, of least things forgotten,
turned from, but sought now, after the bombs.

7

Of solitude, of things human without someone,
your portrayal: Bukovinan? Ukrainian?
or Beatrice? Eurydice? Maybe Anschtel's
mother would recall when you were cast, then placed
in your continuum—the question posed above
a Viennese photographer's prop
in the Hall of Mirrors, where headless
a man and woman in formal dress wave
from the painted buggy. In the amusement park,
cavalry of the First World War trained
as children on the carousel. Perhaps
a few people, living the day you become
a mound of white dust on the pavement,
may remember your resemblances.

8

Few think twice about your presence now.
Your street of poplars remains—snow in each niche.
A house is a division of flats. Behind you
the brick-made space for an intimate life:
your body, part wood, part glass, of the window.
Your form recedes over lamplight in the folds
of curtains. You've never wept nor will—
what we see is snow melting or rain; it finds
the Prut, eventually the Black Sea,
the current of primitive awareness,
the infinite distances as when I stand
among winter trees, as one among ruins. Still
here, the jangling clop of horse and wagon—
Mercedes and Ladas, their engines gunned.

9

Here, in what was once a city of Jews,
I've seen your anonymity reproduced,
unadorned above a garage (a carriage house
standing from the Great War) in the Jewish quarter
near the train tracks not far from Cathedral Square—
the ghetto designated by those in line
after him who made your mold: SS
Einsatskommando 10B of Eisatzgruppe
D. Yet if your house were torched, your eyes, those
darknesses, would be safe from the flames and the dust,
wind-scattered. Adhered, your lineaments of sand,
lime, water and hair are undefiant—
a relic born from a bucket. Your outlasting,
an emblem, fragile as bones at birth.

10

March, late afternoon, beads of moisture
appear on your mask, like sweat from the plaster,
or come to you like dew, like the cries
of a finch from the poplar in its flurry
of seeds drifting down, as snow through dust,
blown across these consequences, things
to come in a dark alive in its depths,
like spring water making its way toward
the surface of a mountain lake, the silt
stirred by rain, the rich dirt washed from shore,
so that we see circles of trapped air
coming like torches of a search party
rising through the night haze, glittering
like a blond Lorelie in a blue sequined dress.

11

Evening, little light remains for the man,
potted, bloodshot, leaning against a wall
near the gypsy extending her open hat
folded from a newspaper. On the bare dirt
of broken pavement, stray pups bunch. Add them
to the watchful: beggars parting from churches;
a cripple on crutches, his thick stump
blunt as a broken carrot, his good leg swaying
like a child's to catch the street; the young woman
in thick-lensed glasses, a cane for her twisted
body—her grimace at each step straightened;
or the tall man standing, his mouth locked gaping,
his loud stutter, his laughter among vendors
closing their flower stalls at Market Square.

12

For the time being all is fixed to a moment.
If only tomorrow's having been were as simple
as yesterday, having survived it. What remains
holds its place in wider circumference—
a form of departure like a crumbling
concrete vacant lot, relinquished. Such wilderness
is a stone age, longed for, nonetheless.
Your severance compels: Let not my house
be squandered. Yet, you have never worried
how long a fabrication can last—
what is loss, if not human? Callused palms
and thick fingers fashioned you with a good time
in mind. . . . To think, whitewash, a few repairs,
the kindness of hands, will keep you.

13

From light's curvatures on the angles
of your pale cast, your parted lips
form a shadow for air, as for a voice
from the timbre of silence, like a beggar
content with a smoke after lunch—fortunate
the length of that cigarette, as on the lips
of the condemned. Clouds thicken in the cold
gray of late afternoon, identified
only by the numbers on my watch.
It is, as said, those with little look up
to you and possess; they know how much
is necessary to hold, but those who
abandon you see only with a brute sense.
Your eyes cannot close. They share the night.

14

Poplar leaves brighten outside my window.
Behind your mask (vernal, suspended there,
where your word waits) ice drips in sunlight
to silence, to the bricks, sun-baked, those
renditions of shape, rough edged, consonant—
each, lodged in mortar, makes the house.
Your body, inherited, embraces your throat.
Part and parcel, hand and trowel formed you,
a witness to what mind has faced and must
(without a mask)—the tide to wrest the rocks
from shore. I feel the warmth of my cup,
the air turned to vapor. Ancient bones,
you know, become a kind of plaster dust;
sand becomes the timber of wind and stone.

NOTES

"Identities": One of Kyiv's earliest settlements, the mercantile quarter of Podol (now Podil) lies on the Dnieper's floodplain, beneath the city's hills.

"The Renovation": Lutsk is an industrial city on the Styr River in northwestern Ukraine. Here, in the fourteenth century, Prince Lubart of Lithuania had a castle built around the ruins of the twelfth-century Church of St. John the Divine. A nineteenth-century painting of St. Agatha is housed in the art museum within the castle.

"From the Ledger of Crossroads": Iaroslav the Wise, son of Volodymyr the Great, ruled Kyivan Rus from 1036 to 1054. Peace prevailed during his reign, when St. Sophia Cathedral was built in 1037. From Iaroslav's death, Kyivan Rus began a process of decline. The Tatars destroyed Kyiv in 1240. Their leader, Batu Khan, boasted, "I will tie Kyiv to the tail of my horse." Michael F. Hamm, *Kiev: A Portrait, 1800–1917*.

"The Blue Cottage": In the countryside surrounding Kraków, there was a tradition of painting the family cottage blue when a girl in the family came of age to marry.

"Tracks": Kontraktova Square is the main square of Podil, where Contract Hall, built in 1817, is centered.

"The Relief": Paul Celan (Paul Antschel, 1920–1970) was born in Czernowitz ("Little Vienna"), Bukovina, present-day Chernivtsi, Ukraine. From 1774, after Turkish rule, Bukovina was a province of the Austro-Hungarian Empire. After World War I, Czernowitz became Romanian Cernauti in 1918. Under the Hitler-Stalin nonaggression pact, Soviets occupied the city in 1940. In 1942, Celan's parents were deported to Transnistria in German-occupied Ukraine. There, Germans shot Celan's mother; his father died of typhus. After Nazi occupation (1941–1944), the city returned as Chernovtsy to Soviet rule in Ukraine. In the tenth through twelfth centuries the area was a stronghold of the Kyivan Rus. N. Pryboya, Alesksei Novikov-Priboi (1877–1944), served in the tsar's navy and wrote a number of sea stories. Victor Terras, *A History of Russian Literature.*

www.ingramcontent.com/pod-product-compliance
Lightning Source LLC
Chambersburg PA
CBHW021349090426
42742CB00008B/790